PLACES *of the* SPIRIT

PRIVATE CHAPEL

Upper St. Regis Lake

Camp built circa 1920

Shellburne Thurber ◆ *Map #29*

Originally built in the 1920s, this camp has been extensively renovated by its current owners. Artistic stonework is common in Adirondack architecture, with its emphasis on the use of natural materials. Massive floor slabs, a heavy bronze door and stately ironwork candleholders create the atmosphere of a hallowed place between lakeside and forest.

PLACES *of the* SPIRIT

SACRED SITES OF THE ADIRONDACKS

THE LAKE PLACID INSTITUTE

Published by The Lake Placid Institute for the Arts and Humanities
P.O. Box 988, 301 Main Street, Third Floor, Lake Placid, NY 12946
www.lakeplacidinstitute.org

ISBN 0-972947-0-0
Printed and bound in Italy by Sfera International, Milan

The Lake Placid Institute Mission & Programs

Founded in 1994, the Lake Placid Institute for the Arts and Humanities seeks to enhance the cultural life of the Adirondack region. We accomplish our mission by shaping an environment that fosters creativity, sharing the talents of world-class artists with the community, developing and sustaining high-quality, innovative programs, forming partnerships with other arts organizations, and celebrating the cultural heritage of the region. Current Institute programs include a series of summer music seminars, an annual conference for writers and illustrators of children's books, a lecture and discussion series featuring experts on global issues, a residency for young playwrights, and a poetry contest for schoolchildren. The Institute welcomes ideas, proposals, volunteers, and supporters of all kinds.

SOURCES CONSULTED

Adirondack Mission Annual Report, 1895-1896. Courtesy of the Adirondack Museum.

De Sormo, Maitland C. Summers on the Saranacs. Saranac Lake, N.Y.: Adirondack Yesteryears, 1980.

Gallos, Phil, Barbara McMartin et al. Discover the Northern Adirondacks. Woodstock, Vermont: Backcountry Publications, 1988.

Gilborn, Craig. Adirondack Camps: Homes Away From Home, 1850-1950. Syracuse, N.Y.: The Adirondack Museum/Syracuse University Press, 2000.

Godine, Amy. "The Hidden History." Adirondack Life (September/October 1993): 46-53, 61-62.

Gordon, Robert. "Days of Ore." Adirondack Life (July/August 1990): 34-38.

Hurd, Duane Hamilton. History of Clinton and Franklin Counties. Philadelphia: J.W. Lewis and Company, 1880.

John, Martha Tyler. "Angel in the Chapel". They Told Me So, Volume I. Quote on p. 77 is from this document.

Johnsburg Historical Society. "A Historical Look at the North Creek Baptist Church." North Creek News-Enterprise (May 4, 2000); "The Methodist Churches." North Creek News- Enterprise (June 22, 2000); "St. Christopher's Episcopal Church." North Creek News-Enterprise (June 15, 2000); "The Wesleyan Methodist Churches." North Creek News-Enterprise (July 6, 2000); "Wevertown Church Named After Cardinal." North Creek News-Enterprise (May 18, 2000).

McGowan, Robert Harold. Architecture From the Adirondack Foothills. New York: Publishing Center for Cultural Resources, 1977. Quote on p. 33 is from p. 98.

Newcomb, Mrs. Elizabeth W. "Stony Wold Sanatorium." Journal of the Outdoor Life (October 1905): 231-232. Quote on p. 28 is from p. 231.

Potter, Junie. A Chapel On an Island. Privately Published, 2002.

Reed, Frank A. Lumberjack Sky Pilot. Old Forge, NY: North Country Books, 1965. Quote on p. 56 is from p. 5.

Seaver, Frederick J. Historical Sketches of Franklin County. Albany, N.Y.: J.B. Lyon and Company, 1918.

Simmons, Lou. Mostly Spruce and Hemlock: Historical Highlights of Tupper Lake and the Town of Altamont. Vail-Ballou Press, Inc, 1976.

Smith, H.P. (Henry Perry). History of Essex County. Syracuse, N.Y.: D. Mason & Co., 1885.

Stonywold Sez. Private Newsletter, December 1951. Courtesy of the Adirondack Museum.

Stonywold Sez. Private Newsletter, March 1954. Courtesy of the Adirondack Museum.

Surprenant, Neil. "The Great Camp No One Knows." Adirondac (May 1989): 21-23.

Talbot, Mary. "Paradise Found." Homestyle (May 1999): 54-65.

Trudeau, Edward Livingston, M.D. An Autobiography. New York: Doubleday, Doran, and Company, 1915. Quote on p. 44 is from p. 127; quote on p. 49 is from p. 80.

Places of the Spirit: Sacred Sites of the Adirondacks is published in conjunction with the exhibition of the same name, curated by Mara Miller for the Lake Placid Institute for the Arts and Humanities.

This project was made possible in part by a grant from the New York State Council on the Arts.

The Lake Placid Institute wishes to thank the following people for their invaluable assistance with this project:

Jerry Pepper, Adirondack Museum Research Staff; Susan Mitchell, Joan Weill Adirondack Library, Paul Smith's College; ; the entire staff of the Saranac Lake Free Library; Louise Patinelli, Lake Placid Public Library; Phil Gallos, North Country Community College Library; Dorothy Irving, Keene Valley Library; Margaret Gibbs and Susan Little, Essex County Historical Society; Mary Hotaling, Historic Saranac Lake; Sally Heidrich and the Johnsburg Historical Society; Father Alan Lamica, St. Brendan's, Keene; Curt and Susan Stiles, Reverend Newton Greiner, and Junie Potter, Island Chapel; Gloria Gori, Duane Methodist; Howard Kirschenbaum, White Pine Camp; Harlan and Kathy Crow; Ralph and Berna Prata; Margo Fish; Ruth Hart; Reverend Milton Dudley and Ruth Pelmas, Keene Valley Congregational; Don and Bettye Muldoon of North Creek; Millie Williams, Uihlein Mercy Center; Janet Chapman, Beth Joseph Synagogue; Sister Teresa and the other Ursuline Sisters at St. Michael's; Father Michael Gaffney, St. Agnes; Reverend Judson Pealer, Nancy Beattie, and Keela Rogers, St. Eustace Episcopal; Reverend Mark Demers and Claire Thayer, Adirondack Community Church; Reverend Alan Macnab, St. James; Dennis Everleth, Essex Senior Center; Andy Bisselle, Camp Dudley; Peter Burns, Orvis Outfitters; Teresa Eshelman, Town Historian for Franklin; Mary MacKenzie, Town Historian for North Elba; Phyllis Bogle, Town Historian for Chester; Betty Tabor, Town Historian for Mayfield; Mary Wallace, Town Historian for Jay; Janice Allen, Town Historian for Willsboro; and Father Douglas Lucia of the Roman Catholic Diocese of Ogdensburg.

ST. JAMES EPISCOPAL CHURCH
Au Sable Forks
Built c. 1925

Romaine Orthwein ◆ *Map #1*

Long after houses ceased to be built in the Gothic Revival style, churches continued to embrace this design. The current church replaces one burned in a fire that swept Au Sable Forks in 1925. It has lancet arched windows, a post-and-beam-type portico, a slate roof, and contrasting sandstone.

FOREWORD

MY SPIRITUAL CONNECTION TO THE ADIRONDACKS BEGAN AT A FAMILY cabin near North Creek when I was no more than a toddler. Even as a child, it wasn't just the magnificent scenery that I responded to, but the deep sense of peace that resides here and serves as both inspiration and tonic. The Adirondacks capture your soul, and once they do, you are drawn back again and again. Those of us who live here year-round are continually blessed with the wild beauty and the pervasive sense of peace that define these mountains, lakes, and small towns.

I like to think of these feelings as a usually unspoken bond with fellow Adirondackers—both now and in the past. The special sites illustrated in these pages are the spiritual expression of those who love this region today and those who came before us.

The Lake Placid Institute began the Sacred Sites project in 1999, inspired by several of the lovely buildings no longer in active use as churches and synagogues. To find these places of the spirit, we turned to the most important resource: the people of the Adirondacks. Requests for information were sent to all 110 towns in the Park, and the result was a plethora of pictures, anecdotes, newspaper articles, pamphlets, and calls offering more assistance. Regional residents are justly proud of their sacred sites, and eager to share them with others.

This is an interdisciplinary project, in keeping with the objectives and approach of the Lake Placid Institute. We wanted to mesh history and art, and produce a traveling photographic exhibition as well as a book that would allow many more people to come to know these sites. Because of this marriage of aesthetics and information, this book is intended neither as a comprehensive history nor as simply an art book. We hope this project will serve as a celebration of our heritage and an inspiration for further preservation and restoration efforts. The term "places of the spirit" is intended to be as encompassing and inclusive as possible. Within these pages you will find not only houses of worship

LOG CABIN CHURCH
Mayfield
Built 1937

Heather MacLeod ◆ *Map #19*

Fifty volunteers built this church in one day, with services of celebration held the next. Everything is made of logs—the walls, ceiling, floors, pews, and chandelier. The building's fireplace is adorned with arrowheads, and the church bell was given by the F.J. and G. Railroad. Today the church serves a non-denominational, year-round congregation.

within the Judeo-Christian tradition, but gravesites, gardens, and places of natural and artistic inspiration.

We thank everyone in the Adirondack Park who helped in the planning and creation of this book. Firstly, we are grateful to the town representatives who took the time to return our surveys and set us on a constant path of discovery; we wish we could have included all of the places you told us about. Early help in selecting possible sites for inclusion also came from Steven Engelhart of Adirondack Architectural Heritage and architectural historian Ted Corbett.

This book, and the exhibition from which it sprang, could not have happened without the extraordinary efforts of the four principal photographers: Barry Lobdell, Heather MacLeod, Romaine Orthwein, and Shellburne Thurber. They were chosen from a wide field of artists who submitted work for our consideration. All of them bring a unique sensibility and style to their subjects, and their contrasts in approach enrich the final product. We are proud to be associated with them. As curator of the show, Mara Miller put in countless hours working on this aspect of the endeavor. She has been involved with the Institute since its founding, and we are deeply grateful for her efforts.

Neil Surprenant of Paul Smith's College and Steven Engelhart and his staff at AARCH offered tireless professional assistance. They provided historical and architectural information, tracked down sources, dug into their archives for rare historical photographs and primary sources, reviewed images, edited captions, and gave marvelous advice.

Many thanks go to Caroline Welsh, Curator of Exhibitions at the Adirondack Museum, and Robbin Zella, Director of the Housatonic Museum of Art, for their support of the exhibition. Thanks also to Margaret Boettcher of North Country Originals in Saranac Lake, who did a superb job framing the exhibition works.

This book would not have been possible without the dedication, good-humor, and gentle criticism of James Lawrence, Alice Lawrence, and Susan McClellan at Microcosm Books in Charlotte, Vermont. John Rosenthal was instrumental in coordinating our publishing plan and in bringing this project to fruition. Without his timely and dedicated assistance, you would not be reading these words. Joan Gignoux generously shared her time and considerable talents as our editor.

Finally, many other members of the Institute's Board of Directors and Advisory Committee assisted in countless ways, from housing photographers and driving them to every corner of the Adirondack Park to offering valuable historical insights. Special thanks go to Adele Connors, Peter Geisler, Jay Higgins, George Hart, George

The Adirondack Community Church in Lake Placid, like so many active places of worship in the region, is a vital hub of spiritual, artistic, and social interaction for local residents and seasonal visitors alike.

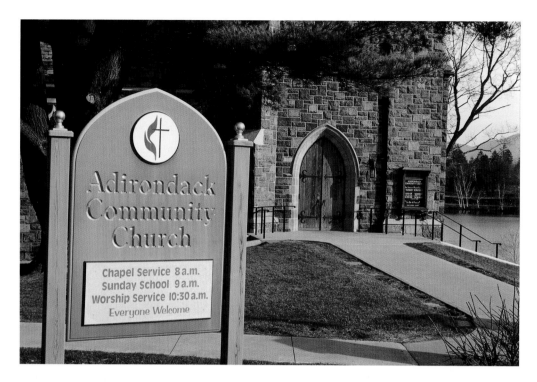

Pappastavrou, James Winn, and the late Robin Pell. Board member Sara Jane DeHoff first conceived of this project, and her advice and support has kept us on track.

Finally, there is one sacred site to which I wish to pay personal tribute. For many years, the Adirondack Community Church has been a valuable supporter and partner to the Institute. They have provided space for master classes and performances for our music program summer after summer. We thank Reverend Mark Demers, Claire Thayer, and the church board for their tireless support. In our view, the Adirondack Community Church embodies some of the best qualities of all of the Adirondack places of the spirit found in these pages: a cheerful welcome to all who come here, great physical beauty, and service to our community.

—*Jennifer Carlo*
Executive Director
Lake Placid Institute for the
Arts and Humanities

INTRODUCTION

THE ADIRONDACK PARK REGION IS BEST KNOWN FOR ITS MILLIONS OF ACRES of wilderness, its rugged mountains, its miles of rivers, and its hundreds of lakes and ponds. Less well known are the region's architectural treasures that represent nearly 250 years of settlement and enterprise in its small communities.

During the late 18th and early 19th centuries, people from New England, Canada, and other parts of New York settled in the region to take advantage of economic opportunities. In the flatter, more fertile valleys, homesteads and farms provided a livelihood for those willing to work the soil. The region's abundant forests were harvested for pulp, paper, lumber, and finished wood products. Wood was also converted into charcoal for making iron in the eastern Adirondacks, and bark from hemlock trees was used for tanning shoe leather. Many kinds of stone were quarried for building, and graphite, garnet, and titanium were mined for a variety of uses.

More than 100 communities formed around these early economic endeavors. Some lasted only as long as the stands of forests or seams of minerals being exploited, and have since disappeared. Some towns adapted to the economic fortunes of their industries and citizens, and remain as small rural settlements rich in history, architecture, and culture.

As communities developed, small groups gathered in homes, barns, and schoolhouses to worship and form religious congregations. Eventually a congregation would erect a church, often at great expense, and requiring great sacrifice. These buildings, often the largest in the community, were placed in prominent locations and endowed with the best available materials and craftsmanship. Today the structures reflect long religious traditions and the aspirations and deep faith of their builders.

The religious buildings of the region reveal an unusual variety and they represent most of the major denominations found in the Northeast: Congregational, Presbyterian, Methodist, Baptist, Episcopal, Catholic, Jewish, United Church of Christ, and Church of

HOLY NAMES OF JESUS AND MARY ORATORY
North Hudson
Built 1893, became Oratory in 1990

Barry Lobdell ◆ Map #22

Shortages of priests in the Roman Catholic Diocese of Ogdensburg have left many parishes without a resident pastor in recent years. Shifting Catholic populations have also left some churches without a surrounding community base. As a result, many historic churches around the Adirondacks are designated as "oratories," a term used for churches that no longer have parishes or regularly scheduled services. Oratories are connected to nearby parishes and can be used for special liturgies, such as weddings, funerals, and parish observances.

the Nazarene. They were built of wood, stone, brick, and concrete block, and ornamented with polished wood, elaborate hammer beams, stained glass, fine fabric and tapestries, brass work, and native rustic materials. Many are simple vernacular buildings or are designed in a variety of architectural styles, such as Federal, Greek Revival, Italianate, Gothic Revival, Queen Anne, and Shingle. They can be found in the village center, on a hillside overlooking the town, hidden deep in the woods, or out on a remote island. A closer examination reveals even more about the faiths that were established in the area, the ethnic traditions of different waves of settlers, the communities in which the buildings are found, and the origins of the church designs.

Designed in a Tudor Revival-style by William L. Coulter, St. Regis Presbyterian Church in Paul Smiths was built in 1899 and was the subject of this vintage postcard.

The region's first wave of permanent settlers, mostly Protestants, arrived after the end of the Revolutionary War and settled primarily in the Champlain Valley. In towns like Lewis and Ironville, Congregationalists from New England built their traditional white clapboard churches in a simple Federal and Greek Revival style. Several Essex County Congregational churches were organized by The Reverend Cyrus Comstock, who was a tireless missionary for the church. Other early nineteenth-century congregations and churches included Baptists, Presbyterians, Methodists and Catholics.

Rapidly growing industries resulted in more economic opportunities. By the last quarter of the nineteenth century, Essex County had become the second largest iron producing region in the country; industrial villages like Keeseville were producing not only nails and boiler plate, but nail-making machinery, pulp, paper, finished wood products, starch, and twine. The demand for skilled and unskilled labor brought new influxes of people into the region and with them, new religious affiliations.

Catholic immigrants from Quebec, Spain, Portugal, and Eastern Europe were the largest new group. Although they settled in communities with existing Catholic churches, the language and established culture were often a barrier to inclusion in the local congregation. In Keeseville, the French-speaking population established St. Jean Le Baptiste in 1853, and bought a small church that the Baptists had outgrown. In 1901, they built a large stone Romanesque Revival church with twin 125-foot towers that was similar to those found in the Quebec countryside.

St. Paul R.C. Church Piercefield, N.Y.

Architectural styles of Adirondack churches display a fascinating range of influences, as exemplified by St. Paul's Roman Catholic Church in Piercefield, photographed circa 1915.

The Beth Joseph Synagogue was built in 1905 by several dozen Jewish families in Tupper Lake. Many of them were Russians who peddled clothing and dry goods in Adirondack lumbering towns and eventually established stores in the village. Beth Joseph was built at a cost of $3526.80 and its form is rooted in Eastern European synagogue design.

In addition to drawing from established cultural traditions, congregations also got their ideas from pattern books, one of the primary nineteenth-century vehicles for popularizing new architectural styles. Richard Upjohn (1802-1878), one of America's pre-eminent architects during the mid-nineteenth century, designed scores of churches, including Trinity Church in New York City. He expressed his architectural vision for young America in his influential 1852 book, *Rural Architecture*, which was the basis for the Boquet Chapel in the Essex County town of Essex. Its board-and-batten siding, steeply pitched roof, and lancet-arched windows closely followed Upjohn's Gothic Revival plans.

As communities in the Adirondacks grew and prospered, they looked to architects to design their buildings. Upjohn's son, Richard Mitchell Upjohn (1828-1903), devoted a major portion of his practice to the design of small, mostly Gothic Revival style churches for Episcopal parishes of modest means in rural areas. He is known to have designed two churches in the Adirondacks: St. Luke's Episcopal Church (1879) in Saranac Lake, and the Church of the Blessed Redeemer (1882) in Bloomingdale.

William L. Coulter (1865-1907), the first professional resident architect of the Adirondacks, designed three churches during his short but prolific career. Baker Chapel (1896), at the former Trudeau Sanatorium in Saranac Lake, where he had been a patient, and the St. Regis Presbyterian Church (1898), near Paul Smiths, still survive today. His successor, William G. Distin (1884-1970), designed the second St. Eustace Episcopal Church (1927) in Lake Placid. Others known to have designed churches in the region include Albany architect Robert W. Gibson, who designed the United Church of Christ (1888) in Elizabethtown, and William Pond, the designer of the Childwold Presbyterian Church (1903) near Tupper Lake. Keeseville native Isaac Perry, the New York State architect credited with completing the State Capitol, designed the Chapel of Our Lady of Perpetual Sorrow at the Sanatorium Gabriels.

PHOTOGRAPH BY H.M. BEACH / COURTESY TED COMSTOCK, SARANAC LAKE

CHURCH OF ALL SAINTS

Mineville

Built 1869

Shellburne Thurber ◆ *Map #20*

Like St. Michael's in Witherbee, the Church of All Saints (formerly St. Peter and Paul's) was established to serve different ethnic groups that came to work in local mines. The church gained its name when several smaller parishes with different patron saints were combined.

St. John's in the Wilderness.   Paul Smith's, N. Y.

Captured in a hand-tinted postcard, St. John's in the Wilderness log church in Paul Smiths was destroyed by fire and replaced by the current stone church, designed by William Distin in 1929 in a rustic traditional style using local materials.

The gradual decline of the region's industries coincided roughly with the rise of tourism in the late nineteenth century, when the Adirondacks became popular for health and recreation. Hotels, boarding houses, private clubs, camps, cabins, liveries, and stores were built to accommodate the visiting public. Among the most permanent and intriguing of these buildings are the dozens of summer churches and chapels that were created for the burgeoning summer population. Many are Episcopal, reflecting the affiliation of many of the region's wealthier summer residents. The Church of the Transfiguration in Blue Mountain Lake was designed by New York architect Manly N. Cutter and built by Thomas Wallace in 1885. This simple log church was built facing the lake, predating the current highway, and most parishioners would have arrived for services by guide boats, canoes, and other watercraft. Saranac Lake architect William G. Distin designed nine churches and chapels, including the Adirondack Community Church (1926) in Lake Placid, and St. John's-in-the-Wilderness (1929) in Paul Smiths. In keeping with the emerging rustic tradition, most of these churches used some combination of stone, logs, and other natural materials for structure and ornamentation.

The region's places of the spirit are by no means limited to the buildings erected by earlier inhabitants. For some, a hike deep into the mountains to see Rainbow Falls flow into its deep chasm, or a canoe trip to see the mist settle around the tea house at White Pine Camp on Osgood Pond is the most profound experience. For others, spiritual nourishment and renewal may be found in a simple altar in the woods, a stone circle in an open meadow, or a recess in a private residence.

It is the wonderful variety of sacred places, large and small, familiar and little known, old and new, that is most astonishing about the Adirondacks. Whether inspiration is to be found in the church of one's grandparents or on a remote mountaintop, the region is blessed with many places that fill the spirit.

—*Steven Engelhart*
Executive Director
Adirondack Architectural Heritage

PLACES OF THE SPIRIT

SACRED SITES OF THE ADIRONDACKS

WHAT CONSTITUTES A SACRED SITE? THIS IS A QUESTION POSED AGAIN and again by the photographers who took pictures of structures and landscapes in the Adirondacks represented in this exhibition. Is a sacred site one in which spiritual activities have occurred? Is a connection with the transcendent a prerequisite for sacredness? Is a connection with death an indicator of the sacred? How does one recognize the sacred in a particular site or landscape?

Sites often become identified as sacred simply because they are a church, synagogue, burial ground, or special area. We also accept the designation of a site as sacred if it has been called sacred by members of our own community, or when it has been designated by political bodies, preservationists, and historians.

The site need not be strictly ecclesiastical, nor must sacred words have been spoken there. Actions such as kneeling, or bowing one's head in silence can be nonverbal indicators of a sacred place. In Native American cultures, including the Mohawk peoples who have always resided in the Adirondacks, a mark, a drawing, or a pictograph can be a concrete reference to a spiritual place.

Sites also become sacred because they contain elements on their own that can be mysterious, spiritual, or what we call "holy." The notion of a transcendent force, or a cataclysmic event, or death as a marker of life comes into play at Ground Zero, Hiroshima, or the Vietnam Memorial Wall. Artists setting out to represent the sacred, on their own terms or on historical terms set by others, often are aware of these standards.

The photograph's capability to capture the ineffable runs deep and permeates the practice of taking pictures. When seeking to define the spiritual, the photographer is challenged to find a quality that cannot be precisely pinpointed or located, and to represent this evanescent quality in an abandoned structure devoid of human presence or a site now adapted for other uses.

Places of the Spirit is presented from the perspectives of architecture, history, and the cultural contexts of particular landscapes and the peoples who inhabit them. The exhibition attempts to show how the sacred may be represented in particular sites or structures, and how the photograph, as both a recorder of the present and a memory of the past, may shed light on issues related to religion, aesthetics, cultural history, art history, and architecture.

The approaches these four photographers have taken towards locating, responding to, and representing the sacredness of physical sites vary enormously. The diversity of these approaches testifies to the array of routes by which one may enter the metaphysical qualities of space and time.

Shellburne Thurber's work merges the spiritual with the emptiness of space and the quality of stillness. *Essex Senior Center* (formerly Methodist-Episcopal Church) (p. 19), which is a photograph of a brilliant green door leading to an exit sign, and a stairway seeming to lead nowhere, conveys a sense of abandonment, even though the structure is an old church in Essex, New York that has been given a second life as a Senior Citizen Center.

Streams of light bathe the interiors of *St. Michael's Roman Catholic Church, Witherbee* (p. 41) and *Church of All Saints, Mineville* (p. 15), but the light never penetrates the entire church. Instead, in the dark, ageless rooms there are only a few indications, like a clock mounted above the confession booth, that both churches function as year-round centers in their communities.

Pews and other furnishings may be an indicator of current use, yet in Thurber's *Church of All Saints, Mineville*, and *Duane Methodist Church* (p. 31), this is deceiving. The former has an active congregation while the latter's Mission-style pews have not been occupied for some years.

The view toward the back interior of *Pottersville Christ Episcopal Church* (p. 39) shows pews that appear old and abandoned, but we recognize immediately the human signs in the bookmarks sticking out from the hymnals, the back doors that don't quite close properly, the wax congealed around the candles, and the books stacked haphazardly on the table.

Thurber photographs this interior as if it were a diorama or dollhouse miniature, emphasizing its small width, foreshortened door and windows, and cropped ceiling. The framing of the shot is slightly askew as well; it is neither composed along a central vertical line, such as the aisle, nor composed horizontally equal from one side wall to the other.

As the photographer Robert Adams said of the photographer Paul Strand, Thurber works "off axis" when she wants to, and always for a reason. Her unorthodox composi-

ESSEX SENIOR CENTER
(Formerly Methodist-Episcopal Church)
Essex
Built 1835

Shellburne Thurber ◆ Map #10

The oldest church in Essex and now owned by the town, this simple Gothic Revival church has recently been partially restored. The lancet windows, typical of Gothic architecture, and the surrounding stonework are the building's most notable features.

tion of an interior or an exterior view seen through an open window seems informed by the black and white landscapes of Strand. In *Pottersville Episcopal*, effects such as stillness and holiness contrast with sunlight, imperfections, and quirky decorations. This church seems lived in by people of an actual community, though there is no human figure to be seen.

The photographer captures the duality of sacred structures in the Adirondacks. These buildings served as places in which to escape the hardships of daily life, and places in which to locate a higher Being, but they also served as vital gathering places for the entire community.

Thurber's *Van Santvoord Room, Keene Valley Community Church* (p. 75), signifies a place of daily use with its open doors and the five Windsor-style chairs placed next to one another, as if a group or panel of church elders had just left and might return shortly. The large landscape mural of the High Peaks, the modern brass chandelier, and the straw waste-basket peeping out from just beyond the corner of the doorway, "paint" a picture of a place that seems open, accessible, and nonecclesiastical. Because there is no recognizable sacred icon in this scene, it looks like an active community room.

Of contrast is the artist's interior view of *Wevertown United Methodist Church* (p. 73), in which solemn religious signifiers are visible: an altar, a crucifix, hymn board, altar railing and stained-glass window, juxtaposed with contemporary decoration, such as plaid wall-paper, wall-to-wall red carpeting, a white garden cornice, and a modern ceiling fixture. In this work, as in the others, Thurber posits the photographer's dilemma of how to represent the sacred in our architecture, in our signs or objects, and in our photographic representations.

The tension in photographic representations of sacred sites occurs between the sense of permanence and the appearance of decline. At the same time that churches, synagogues, burial grounds, and even sublime landscapes stand for the permanent, dignified, and eternal, they can also serve as signifiers of rapid change, transformation, and extinction.

Heather MacLeod is an artist from Halifax, Nova Scotia, who works primarily in black and white silver gelatin prints, and whose past landscape photographs have emphasized the horizontal planes of her native country's terrain. Her sacred site images, by contrast, are in a square format, in which the structures or sites are centered, both vertically and horizontally. *Former Episcopal Summer Church, Franklin Falls* (p. 21) fills the entire frame so that the steeple of the church, now a store, marks the center of the image precisely.

MacLeod's photographs of Adirondack structures foreshorten both foreground and

FORMER EPISCOPAL SUMMER CHURCH
(Now a store)
Franklin Falls

Many historic places of worship throughout the Adirondacks have been adapted for other uses when they were no longer needed by congregations. Some were converted to homes, while others were put into commercial use.

Heather MacLeod ◆ Map #11

middle ground, so that holy or sacred objects are viewed head-on. Churches usually photographed from some distance, whether deep foreground to background, or from the ground up toward the steeple, loom larger and seem more dominant than they actually may be in their communities.

MacLeod also places her subjects in a contemporary context, revealing the power lines that crisscross the view of the steeple in *North Creek First Baptist Church* (p. 62), the basketball hoop in the backyard of *Log Cabin Church, Mayfield* (p. 8), or the massive cement garden bench in front of *Virgin Mary Shrine, Keene* (p. 50).

Photographs are also central to the process of remembering. MacLeod's choice of the square black and white format gives back the permanence and dignity that the usual contextual placement attempts to deny. *St. Christopher's Church, North Creek* (p. 58), which is not in the exhibition but included in this book, appears to have been taken from an old album of the 1930's. The amazing white light of the small church, the crucifix on its steeple, its signboard, and the one cloud in the sky, evoke an earlier time in Adirondack history when small communities worshiped quietly, and a cross or a steeple was all that was needed to signify a sacred site. The photograph here transforms itself into an image of the present and a memory of the past.

MacLeod's images refer to The Farm Security Administration photographs of the 1930's, made by such artists as Walker Evans, Marion Post Wolcott, and Dorothea Lange, which depicted the impoverished lives and buildings of Appalachia and the Southeast, while at the same time investing these subjects with dignity and distinction.

The history of artistic practice that informs Barry Lobdell's pictures of sacred sites in the Adirondacks is more complex. Lobdell is a native of the region as well as a professional photographer. As a long-time resident, he is highly aware of how this particular landscape has been represented by world-renowned artists such as Kensett, Coleman, Durand, and Jackson, and how the landscape has been represented conventionally in calendars, postcards, posters, and greeting cards.

He also knows the landscape and history of the area better than the other photographers in this exhibition. He knows that as high as Whiteface Mountain is, there is never a cloud around any part of it other than the very top. He knows that fog still envelops the eastern Adirondack lakes such as Placid, the Saranacs, or Upper St. Regis until about 7:30 in the morning, so this is also the time when the fish rise and fishermen will appear (see *Teahouse, White Pine Camp, Paul Smiths*, p. 43). And he knows that no matter what the weather may be at a given moment, it is apt to change quickly, so the

ST. BRENDAN'S ROMAN CATHOLIC CHURCH
Keene
Built 1883

Barry Lobdell ◆ Map #15

Many Adirondack churches were named for patron saints of particular interest to the ethnic groups they served. St. Brendan the Voyager was a sixth-century Irish missionary. Shortly after the conversion of Ireland to Christianity, Brendan and 60 other monks set out on a voyage to North America to spread the word of their new faith. Contemporary legends from Ferro, Gomera, Madeira, and the Azores hold that when Columbus and his crew arrived they were told of the Irish missionaries by the area's native inhabitants. After his return, Brendan founded numerous churches, monasteries, and dioceses in Britain, Wales, and Ireland. The main altar of this church is hand-carved with a sixth-century ship and two swords to commemorate St. Brendan.

photographer who wants to capture a particular mood or effect of a site must be patient.

In *St. Brendan's Catholic Church, Keene* (p. 23), Lobdell has waited for just that moment when the daylight departs the northern windows of the church, leaving one last orb of yellow light on the floor. In *Church of the Nazarene, Vermontville* (p. 77), he waited for a clear evening just after sunset to be able to capture the stained-glass angel as a golden floating apparition.

The simple, graceful Romanesque structure of *Duane Methodist Church* (p. 30) was photographed on an early fall day, when cold, dry air from the West had blown all the clouds from the sky, leaving a brilliant canvas of bright blue that contrasts with the red of the steeple and the gray stone foundation. When the landscape photographer Ansel Adams passed the town of Hernandez, New Mexico, he saw an "extraordinary situation" for a photograph but could not find his exposure meter. Suddenly he realized he knew the luminance of the moon $(250c/ft^2)$, and this improvisation resulted in one of his most famous photographs. Lobdell also knows instinctively how light can be measured in the Adirondacks at a given moment on a given day.

Lobdell understands the culture of the Adirondacks, its habits and traditions. In *Soldier's Monument, Wevertown* (p. 48), the combination of the bronze military grave plaque, the bucolic Adirondack landscape backdrop, and the artificiality of the red, white, and blue flowers forced into shapes of giant wreaths, results in a moving portrait of one individual's death and another individual's marking of it. The image is a small window into another world. *Garden with Tibetan Prayer Flags, Bloomingdale* (p. 71), could only have been taken by someone who knows that the artist Ralph Prata has such a garden and that it holds such symbols of faith.

Romaine Orthwein digitally manipulates her subject matter, thus creating her own scenes in her works. Her approach to the representation of sacred places is to insert herself, either physically or digitally into her photographs; it is not clear if the resulting image indicates an ineffable presence or an unwitting bystander. Orthwein's work reflects a postmodern deliberate insistence that landscapes and interiors have little meaning without human reference, but she does not settle for the small signs of human presence like hymnal bookmarks or empty chairs in a circle.

In *Private Chapel, Tapawingo* (p. 25), the artist, in a white dress, is visible through the glass window of the tiny chapel in the woods. The woman's image is enigmatic. It is uncertain if she is praying or even if she is a real figure, because the reflection of the landscape in the glass makes the figure appear headless, as if it was an apparition. The

TAPAWINGO CHAPEL

Private Chapel

Camp Tapawingo

Lake Placid

Romaine Orthwein ♦ Map #18

"The word sacred is a link between the abstract connection of the Holy or the mystery of creation and a living experience," says the camp's creator. "Tapawingo is Mohawk and means 'House of Joy.' Made from free pine siding, the chapel emerged as students and friends dreamed with us and asked if their weddings or their babies' baptisms could take place at Tapawingo. The chapel holds symbols from most religions of the world. As in nature, boundaries and dogmas disappear. Perhaps a little chapel in the Adirondacks is an open spirit for the sacred to be perceived."

contrast is between the human figure as an earth signifier and the human figure as stand-in for a spiritual presence.

Orthwein's photographs force the viewer to ask questions about the content and meaning of her images. What is that woman doing in a white dress, barefoot, heading toward the door of the church on *Chapel Island* (p. 27)? What is that woman looking up toward, in the doorway of *St. James Episcopal Church, Au Sable Forks* (p. 6)? The images also pose questions about the sites themselves. Can just anyone go to Chapel Island? What goes on in that private chapel with its outdoor chairs and tables and a piano dimly seen inside?

One can argue that these are the questions we ought to be asking about the sacred or spiritual sites in the Adirondacks, and in our own communities, if we are to decide whether to preserve, readapt, or abandon them. The artist herself is standing in for the viewer who cannot ask such questions when confronting a church or temple that is cloaked in signifiers of reverence such as stillness, crosses or steeples.

In *Beth-Joseph Synagogue, Tupper Lake* (p. 34), the artist could be an apparition, but she could also be a real person, a stand-in for us. By contrast, in Orthwein's photograph of *St. Eustace, Lake Placid* (p. 29), the church seems an empty uninhabited shell without the artist or another human figure.

Orthwein's images bring to the surface consideration of the conditions under which spiritual sites might operate if they are to survive as more than quaint artifacts or landmarks. If the spiritual once inhabited these spaces but does so no more, or if these sites contain deeper and more permanent meanings than their worn surfaces imply, such spaces will only survive the rapid changes of a community if the human figure is made a factor once again.

This does not necessarily mean a return to weekly churchgoing, nor does it mean a reliance on the divisions that separate one religion from another. It may mean instead a regard for certain places based on the lives they historically touched, and can continue to touch, among all members of their communities.

—*Mara Miller*
Exhibition Curator

CHAPEL ISLAND
Upper Saranac Lake
Current chapel built 1958

Romaine Orthwein ◆ Map #28

Chapel Island was given in 1892 to the Champlain Presbytery by three Plattsburgh attorneys. The first chapel on the Island was built in 1889 in the Victorian style and rebuilt after a fire in 1956. The large birch cross is a landmark for boaters on Upper Saranac Lake. Over the years island families and their guests, as well as students from the Union Theological Seminary, have filled the role of visiting minister. Today many local and guest ministers of all denominations lead worship each summer on a rotating basis. (See also page 42.)

**CHURCH OF THE WHITE FATHERS
OF AFRICA**
(Originally Potter Memorial)
Lake Kushaqua
Built 1906-1920

Heather MacLeod ◆ *Map #17*

Stony Wold Sanatorium was founded in 1903 by Elizabeth Newcomb for the benefit of children and young women suffering from tuberculosis. In 1905 Ms. Newcomb described the site she had chosen: "From its vantage point, sixty feet above the lake, it commands an unbroken view of woodland and mountain readily suggesting the meaning of the Indian word 'kushaqua,' 'beautiful resting place,' as it also suggested to its present occupants the name 'Stony Wold,' 'wold' in old English meaning an elevated tract of woodland where hunters fish and roam." Stony Wold was sold to the missionary White Fathers of Africa, a Roman Catholic order in the 1950s. The state bought the property in the 1970s and destroyed many of the buildings, but the Elizabethan Revival chapel was left standing.

ST. EUSTACE EPISCOPAL CHURCH
Good Shepherd Window
Lake Placid
Church Built 1900, Moved 1927

Romaine Orthwein ♦ Map #18

The Episcopal congregation in Lake Placid began in 1894 in the parlor of the Stevens House Hotel. A small gothic church, St.-Eustace-By-the-Lakes, was built in 1900. In 1927 the church was torn down, its boards numbered, and reassembled on its present site. The current church has a 60 foot stone tower, stained cedar siding, and a butt heart cedar roof. The altar and baptismal font are made of wood and are from the original church. The rustic wrought iron lamps were hand-hammered in nearby Au Sable Forks, and the needlepoint kneelers throughout the church were handmade by the women of the congregation. The windows in St. Eustace are among its most famous features. The three panel St. Eustace Window, the small circular Lee Memorial Window, and a window over the door leading into the church are all thought to have been made in the Tiffany Studios. Other beautiful memorial windows have been given by parishioners over the years. The one pictured above is known as the Good Shepherd Window.

DUANE METHODIST CHURCH
Duane
Built 1884, Used until 1982

Barry Lobdell ◆ Map #8

The Duane Methodist Episcopal Church overlooks the former Port Kent to Hopkinton Turnpike. Its plain rectilinear exterior is in stark contract to its rich, warm interior. Although no longer in use, the building is listed on the National Register of Historic Places. (See opposite page.)

DUANE METHODIST CHURCH
Duane
Built 1884, used until 1982

Shellburne Thurber ◆ Map #8

The stillness of this church remains a testament to the early efforts of James Duane, for whom the Township of Duane was named in 1828, and for whom most of the men in the township then worked. Mr. Duane, a grandson of New York City's first mayor, came to the North Country to settle on lands inherited by his wife. Among the businesses he created were a brick kiln, a sawmill, a mine, and a forge. In the town's earliest years he and his wife built a school, led prayer meetings, dispensed medical care, and did whatever they could to look after the early settlers.

CHURCH OF THE TRANSFIGURATION
Blue Mountain Lake
Built 1885

Barry Lobdell ◆ *Map #4*

Founded by summer visitors to Blue Mountain Lake, this church maintains the area's tradition of using natural materials and rustic design. Small, with a gable roof and a central belfry, it has two rear rooms that create a cross-like layout. The church was built on the lakeside to allow worshippers to arrive by boat. Tiffany Studios reputedly made the stained glass windows. The church is listed on the National Register of Historic Places.

STAINED GLASS WINDOW
Church of the Angel Gabriel
Paul Smiths
Built circa 1896, became
Oratory in 2002

Barry Lobdell ◆ Map #23

All of the windows in this small
church are stained glass, beautifully
setting off the rich wood paneling of
the interior. Historian Robert
McGowan commented that "whoever
matched and finished these walls
loved the patterns that wood grains
make. The paneling startles one with
its dark richness, with its contrast to
the white exterior."

St. Gabriel's stained glass windows
were restored by parish volunteers
with the help of a local artist in the
church's complete restoration in
1994-95.

BETH JOSEPH SYNAGOGUE

Tupper Lake

Built 1905

Romaine Orthwein ◆ *Map #27*

The Tupper Lake Jewish congregation was the first in the Adirondacks and formed in the 1890s. Families from Lake Placid, Franklin Falls, Paul Smith's Station, Bloomingdale, and Buck Mountain joined in for minyan (a group of ten adult men traditionally required for a prayer service) and yartzeit (memorial service said on the anniversary of a parent's death). The congregation was originally called Beth Anshey; the name was changed to Beth Joseph with the building of the synagogue in 1905. (See opposite page and page 65.)

JUDAICA
Beth Joseph Synagogue
Tupper Lake

Shellburne Thurber ♦ *Map #27*

Those involved with the painstaking restoration of this synagogue have described the building and its history as a "gift to us from the past." The first Jewish settlers in the Adirondacks, most of them immigrants from Eastern Europe, were peddlers of small household goods who traveled between local homes and logging camps. The community waited to build this synagogue until Tupper Lake had recovered from its catastrophic 1899 town fire, which burned 165 homes, to be assured that local jobs and vitality would continue. (See opposite page and page 65.)

UNITED CHURCH OF CHRIST

Elizabethtown

Built 1889

Romaine Orthwein ◆ Map #9

The First Congregational Church of Elizabethtown was organized in 1821 by the Reverend Cyrus Comstock. "Father" Comstock, as he was known, worked with the Berkshire Missionary Society of Massachusetts and founded several other churches in the area as well. (He also invented the Comstock buckboard wagon.) The congregation erected the handsome stone church seen today in 1889. After merging with local Methodists in the 1930s and with a Baptist congregation in 1957, the church became the home of the United Church of Christ.

CURVED PEWS
United Methodist Church
Willsboro
Built 1891

Shellburne Thurber ◆ Map #33

The Methodist Congregation in Willsboro was first established in 1830 and has held services continuously for more than 170 years. Their first church was a brick structure built in 1846 and torn down in 1891 because of foundation cracks. Construction began immediately on the present church. The warm oak pews and wainscoting are original and were restored in 1970.

GOOD SHEPHERD EPISCOPAL
CHURCH
Chestertown
Built 1881

Heather MacLeod ◆ Map #5

Fire is not an uncommon part of the history of Adirondack churches. Church of the Good Shepherd was gutted by a blaze but promptly restored in 1926-27.

POTTERSVILLE CHRIST EPISCOPAL CHURCH
Pottersville
Built 1925

Shellburne Thurber ◆ Map #24

Early Adirondack settlers who belonged to the Church of England wanted their own house of worship and incorporated this congregation in 1844. The property on which the church stands was a gift, and work began on a church immediately. The first services were held the following year and the bell tower added in 1860. The first wood frame church burned in 1925 and was immediately rebuilt. In 1959 the church came under the jurisdiction of the Adirondack Missions. Many of the small Episcopal churches left in the region today lack a pastor or a large enough congregation to stand alone as parishes, so the Missions, based at Barry House in Brant Lake, jointly administer several of them.

SHRINE OF THE SACRED HEART OF JESUS

St. Catherine of Siena Roman Catholic Oratory
Clintonville
Built 1825, became Oratory in 1955

Barry Lobdell ◆ *Map #7*

In 1871 the Peru Iron and Steel Company deeded the property on which St. Catherine's now sits, with its existing building, to the Irish Catholic Society of Clintonville. The parish was incorporated in 1875. The statue, dedicated in 1925, was given by parishioners and friends to commemorate the 100th anniversary of the building and the 50th anniversary of the parish.

As with other Catholic churches that no longer hold regular services and have been named as oratories, the future of properties such as this and St. Michael's on the opposite page are uncertain. If, after a church has been designated an oratory for five years, there remains no perceived need for services to be held there on an ongoing basis, the Diocese may allow the local parish to sell the building or convert it to other uses.

ST. MICHAEL'S ROMAN CATHOLIC
CHURCH
Witherbee
Built 1912

Shellburne Thurber ◆ *Map #35*

Mining in the Moriah area attracted many European immigrants eager for work in the latter half of the nineteenth century. Large French and Irish Catholic communities were thriving there when Eastern and Southern Europeans began to arrive in the mid-1890s. Poles and other Eastern Europeans felt unwelcome in the existing church and wanted their own sacred space. The Witherbee-Sherman Company, which employed a great number of these newer immigrants, gave land and money to build St. Michael's. The church was built from concrete blocks pressed from the company's iron ore tailings. Many large companies of the era held an encompassing attitude toward their workers' needs, and built housing, churches, and other structures in these new communities.

CHAPEL ISLAND
Upper Saranac Lake
Current chapel built 1958

Romaine Orthwein ◆ *Map #28*

One of the distinguishing features of this chapel is its large, clear glass window over the altar to showcase the natural landscape. (See exterior view, page 27.) The birch cross on the west of the Island is at least the third erected by regular worshippers; the current cross was placed in 1995. Lumberjack sky pilot Aaron Maddox served as the first minister for both Chapel Island and nearby Indian Carry Chapel. Chapel Island is continually maintained by dedicated volunteers.

TEAHOUSE, WHITE PINE CAMP
Paul Smiths
Camp built 1907

Barry Lobdell ◆ *Map #23*

In the early twentieth century, the Whites of White Pine Camp were notable patrons of New York opera and hosted many musicians of great distinction. One morning, two sisters who summered near White Pine ventured out onto a foggy lake for an early canoe ride. As they paddled through the early morning quiet, they heard a voice, singing with passion, ringing from the trees and water. They paddled closer, following the music through the mist, and the voice grew louder. Drawn in by the beauty of the music and the morning, they followed the sound to a guideboat, with a single passenger, intent on his private dawn rehearsal.

It was Enrico Caruso.

TRUDEAU FAMILY GRAVES
St. John's in the Wilderness
Episcopal Cemetery
Paul Smiths

Barry Lobdell ◆ Map #23

St. John's in the Wilderness was founded by Dr. Edward Livingston Trudeau and fellow Paul Smith's guests as a small log chapel. The land and the logs were donated by Paul Smith, and such other accoutrements as windows, chairs, bells, and altar pieces were contributed by other guests and friends. Dr. Trudeau regarded the building of this church as "the beginning of a lifetime of begging money from my friends, an occupation I have carried on unceasingly." The church was consecrated in 1877 and enlarged in 1893. The original church burned in 1928 and was replaced the next year by a stone structure that remains in seasonal use. The new church features buttressed walls, more than 20 stained glass windows, and a slate roof with a witch's peak.

Several generations of the Trudeau family lie at rest in the adjoining graveyard.

STONE MONUMENT AND GRAVES

Duane

Shellburne Thurber ◆ Map #8

In the Adirondacks, cemeteries are far more likely to have evolved from necessity rather than by a landscape architect's design. Elaborate monuments and mausoleums are rare, but in some instances families were able to go to great lengths and sacrifice to erect memorials to their departed loved ones.

OVERGROWN GRAVESITE
Wilmington

Shellburne Thurber ♦ Map #34

"A graveyard, for me, is the perfect place to connect with my spiritual self," says one contemporary Wilmington resident. "You feel a connection with everyone before you and a common bond with everyone to come; the impermanence of this world is the one thing we all share. In the Adirondacks, there's a vivid contrast with the rugged mountain peaks rising all around you. Those are permanent. The rivers and the lakes form part of a perfect chain between the past, present, and future that can't easily be seen when you're surrounded with human-made landscapes. Whether you believe in God, the spirit world, or another Higher Power, you'll find it here."

STONE WITH CARVED CROSS

Gravesite

Duane

Shellburne Thurber ◆ Map #8

As one drives along the backroads and even the major highways of the Adirondacks, small groups of gravesites can be glimpsed from time to time. Sometimes they are small family plots in which all the graves are more than a hundred years old.

BROKEN STONE WITH HAND

Gravesite

Wilmington

Shellburne Thurber ◆ Map #34

Some of those buried in these plots may have no descendants remaining in the Adirondacks, leaving no one to tend their graves; other sites show signs of continuing, loving care. In some jurisdictions, town governments or historical societies have assumed these responsibilities.

REVOLUTIONARY WAR GRAVE
Jay

Barry Lobdell ◆ Map #13

Robert Otis, "a soldier of the War of the Revolution," was an early settler and one of the first supervisors of the Town of Jay.

SOLDIER'S MONUMENT
Gravesite
Wevertown

Barry Lobdell ◆ Map #32

Men from the Adirondacks have served in all of America's wars. Old town histories, memorial boards in churches and high schools, and monuments throughout the Park pay tribute to their sacrifices.

ST. JOHN'S IN THE WILDERNESS

St. John the Baptist Statue

Paul Smiths

Church built 1929

Heather MacLeod ◆ Map #23

Dr. Edward Livingston Trudeau arrived at the Paul Smith's resort in June 1873 seeking "the magic influence of the surroundings" as a respite from his recently-diagnosed tuberculosis. He gained such wonderful results that he remained, and founded the Adirondack Cottage Sanitarium in 1884, followed by the Saranac Laboratory for the Study of Tuberculosis. Dr. Alfred Loomis, inspired by Dr. Trudeau's progress and that of a few other hardy souls who ventured into the remote Adirondacks for health reasons, first recommended the region's climate for pulmonary patients in The Medical Record in 1876. For the next eighty years tubercular patients flocked to Saranac Lake and surrounding communities to "take the cure." He helped to found the original St. John's in the Wilderness in 1877. After a catastrophic fire in 1928, the current church was rebuilt the following year. It is still in use seasonally.

VIRGIN MARY SHRINE
Our Lady of Grace Shrine, St. Brendan's
Roman Catholic Church
Keene
Consecrated 1957

Heather MacLeod ◆ Map #15

Originally consecrated in 1957, this outdoor shrine received a new statue as a gift from two parishioners in celebration of the church's 100th anniversary in 1982.

YOUNG PERSON'S GRAVE

Bates Cemetery

Johnsburg

Shellburne Thurber ◆ Map #14

ST. WILLIAM'S ROMAN CATHOLIC CHURCH
Raquette Lake
Built 1939

Barry Lobdell ◆ Map #25

The first St. William's Church in Raquette Lake was built in 1890 on Long Point and moved into the village in 1928. A fire in 1938 destroyed the church, and the current structure was rebuilt the next year.

CHURCH OF THE ANGEL GABRIEL
Paul Smiths
Built circa 1896, became Oratory in 2002

Barry Lobdell ◆ Map #23

St. Gabriel's was built on land donated by Paul Smith and was originally intended to serve the many Catholics who worked in Smith's various business ventures. Over time the church was also used for some campus ministries at Paul Smith's College. The building has flared eaves, clapboard and scalloped shingle siding, a belvedere, and a steeple, whose shingles alternate between simple and fish scale. The interior is finished with beaded tongue-and-groove paneling, with the grain of the interior wood arranged in patterns to complement the natural surroundings. The building was completely restored in 1994-95.

POTTERSVILLE UNITED
METHODIST CHURCH
Pottersville
Built 1847

Heather MacLeod ◆ *Map #24*

This congregation is one of the oldest in the Adirondacks, organized in 1810. At that time ministers traveled from site to site on horseback, saying services in private homes. On the frontier, as Northern New York was then, the minister's regular visits were much anticipated. (See opposite page.)

**POTTERSVILLE UNITED
METHODIST CHURCH**
Pottersville
Built 1847

Shellburne Thurber ◆ Map #24

This pre-Civil War Church was thoroughly remodeled in 1884. Although the memorial hall (1940) and steeple (1970) have been added more recently, much of the church structure remains as it was in the nineteenth century. (See exterior, opposite.)

FORMER INDIAN CARRY CHAPEL
(Now a private residence)
Harrietstown
Built 1888

Barry Lobdell ◆ Map #12

Preachers who traveled between lumber camps in the late nineteenth and early twentieth centuries were known as sky pilots, a term derived from an early minister's ambition "to pilot men to the skies!"

The Reverend Aaron Maddox, who came to the Tupper Lake area in 1900 to take the tuberculosis cure, assumed responsibility for the "lumber camp parish" in 1914 and found the task so huge that he continually recruited other ministers to join him. In his 1915 report, Maddox tells of visiting more than 125 camps in an area that spanned 11 counties. As the number of lumber camps dropped during and after the Depression, Maddox continued his itinerant ministry among small churches and chapels in rural areas.

This beautifully proportioned chapel was originally built as part of the sky pilot program and is said to have been founded by Reverend Maddox himself.

CAMP DUDLEY
OUTDOOR CHAPEL
Westport
Camp established 1885

Romaine Orthwein ◆ *Map #31*

Camp Dudley is the oldest continuously operating boys' camp in the country. Noted actor Burgess Meredith got his start on the Camp Dudley stage in the late 1920s, and would have graced the chapel as well. YMCA-affiliated, the camp operates within the Christian tradition but respects and welcomes all faiths. Services are held in the outdoor chapel every Sunday at noon during the eight-week summer season. The camp's motto is "The Other Fellow First," and that tradition remains the heart and soul of camp life.

ST. CHRISTOPHER'S EPISCOPAL
CHURCH
North Creek
Built 1948

Heather MacLeod ◆ *Map #21*

Adirondack congregations, faced with remote locations and often little money, have learned to adapt and innovate when constructing their sacred spaces. St. Christopher's was built from a prefabricated garage, assembled by volunteers on donated land. The steeple was built by a church member in his basement. The congregation remains the smallest in the Episcopal Diocese of Albany.

BIBLE IN RECTORY
Church of All Saints
Mineville

Shellburne Thurber ◆ Map #20

When churches are redesignated as oratories or otherwise fall into disuse, Adirondack congregations have proved remarkably adaptable. This antique bible sits in what was first a rectory. After the parish no longer had a resident priest, the building became known as the "Parish House." Now that the church is no longer a parish, those who served the community's needs have adapted once again. The Ursuline Sisters now in residence here say, "Our ministry in Mineville and Witherbee is primarily one of presence—meeting people where they are, on the streets, at the post office, at the store."

CHILDWOLD
PRESBYTERIAN CHURCH
Childwold
Church built 1903

Barry Lobdell ◆ *Map #6*

*The town of Childwold was named
for founder Addison Child, who gave
land to the Champlain Valley
Presbytery to build this church.
(See opposite page.)*

**MEMORIAL PRESBYTERIAN
CHURCH**
Childwold
Built 1903

Barry Lobdell ◆ Map #6

Currently used seasonally, this one-story church has several notable architectural details, including its prominent bellcast steeple and center rosette, multipaned windows, decorative shingle patterns, and large wall dormers. (See opposite page.)

NORTH CREEK FIRST BAPTIST
CHURCH
North Creek
Built 1853

Heather MacLeod ◆ *Map #21*

The Town of Johnsburg Historical Society lists the First Baptist Church as only the fourth building erected within the township. The congregation was founded in 1838 by Elder Josiah Wetherby. A tiered graveyard dating back to the eighteenth century is located adjacent to the church.

UNITED METHODIST CHURCH
Johnsburg
Built 1843

Shellburne Thurber ◆ Map #14

The mural behind the altar of this church was painted by former pastor Anton Beza in 1942. Before entering the ministry, Beza designed carpets and stained glass, and he was determined to utilize his artistic talents in his new calling. Measuring 10 feet by 12 feet, his mural depicts Jesus as a shepherd with a view of Crane Mountain, as seen from the church's door, in the background. Stained glass memorial windows line the walls.

UIHLEIN MERCY CENTER
Lake Placid
Built 1968

Romaine Orthwein ◆ Map #18

Henry Uihlein II, a local benefactor, donated land and formed a steering committee to build this facility, which opened in 1968. Affiliated with the Catholic Church but ecumenical in its approach, Uihlein has a number of spiritual elements. The cross on top of the building was designed by Adé Bethune, with the Terra Sancta Guild in Newport, Rhode Island. Bethune also created the main chapel inside, which features pyramidal windows symbolizing the houses of the people of God and a main window with symbols for the Holy Trinity. Decorative mosaic work, with 12 birds to symbolize the 12 apostles, and a Russian-style icon were also created by Bethune for the building's interior.

BETH JOSEPH SYNAGOGUE

Tupper Lake

Built 1905

Shellburne Thurber ◆ *Map #27*

The windows in this restored building are original and feature colors that delicately blend around the edges. The pews, bema (altar), chandeliers, and light fixtures are all original. Fir wainscoting lines the building's interior. The exterior shows a distinct Eastern European influence that is unique to the region, reflecting the origins of most of the first Jewish settlers to the Adirondacks. This is the oldest synagogue in the Adirondacks and is listed on the National Register of Historic Places. (See also pages 34-35.)

**ST. BRENDAN'S CATHOLIC
CHURCH**
Keene
Built 1883

Romaine Orthwein ◆ *Map #15*

In its earliest years, St. Brendan's was served by priests from surrounding parishes in Elizabethtown, Westport, Keeseville, Plattsburgh, and Au Sable Forks. Mass was held in the nearby Manning Homestead before the church was built in 1883 with materials donated by parishioners and other parishes. The original stained glass windows are thought to have come from a refurbished church in Mineville. The walls are paneled in oak, and the altars, pulpit lectern, and statue pedestals are all seasoned oak, hand-carved by a craftsman from nearby Upper Jay. (See opposite page.)

ST. BRENDAN'S CONFESSION BOOTH
St. Brendan's Catholic Church
Keene

Romaine Orthwein ◆ *Map #15*

Like so many religious sites in the Adirondacks, St. Brendan's has gone through numerous renovations and changes over the years. The screen shown on the wall of this confession booth leads to nothing; the half of the booth where a penitent once knelt has long since been blocked off and a statue placed behind it. The rest of the booth is scheduled to be eliminated in another planned renovation in 2003-04. (See opposite page.)

RIVERSIDE EPWORTH
LEAGUE
Riparius
Established 1873

Barry Lobdell ✦ *Map #26*

Religious meeting places, modeled on Chautauqua in Western New York, were common in the late nineteenth century. The Reverend Aaron Hall led a group in the founding the The Riverside Campmeeting Association in 1873 along the Hudson River. Preachers stood on raised platforms; worshippers gathered around in wagons, on stumps, or on the ground. (See opposite page.)

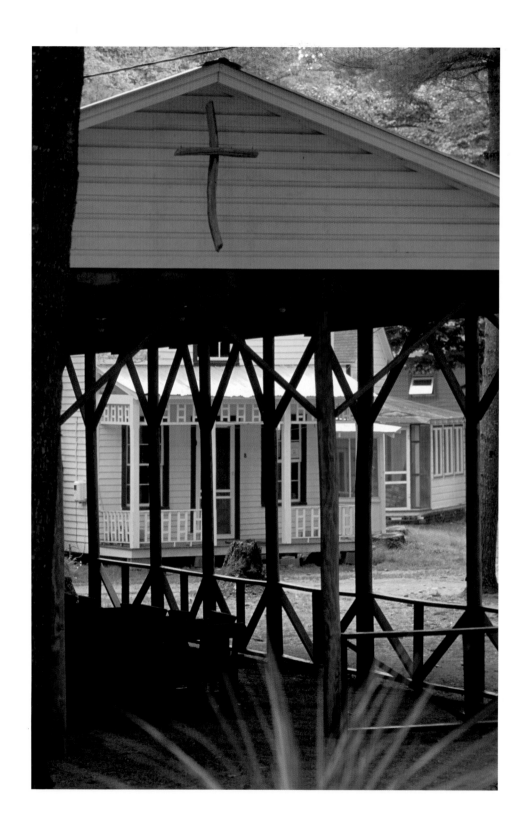

READING ROOM, RIVERSIDE EPWORTH LEAGUE

Riparius

Established 1873

Shellburne Thurber • Map #26

At times as many as 3,000 people may have gathered here, some of whom built tents for longer visits. Cottages were eventually constructed as well. Public services are still held at the campground during the summer, and this reading room continues to provide a quiet place to find a good book or escape a rainy day. (See opposite page.)

PRIVATE GARDEN, ORIGINAL SITE
OF ST. EUSTACE-BY-THE-LAKES
EPISCOPAL CHURCH
Lake Placid
Church built 1900, moved 1927

Romaine Orthwein ◆ Map #18

When the chapel called St. Eustace-by-the-Lakes was torn down and rebuilt on Main Street in 1927, the church's original foundation and grounds were transformed by an unknown gardener into a commemorative landscape. By 1972, however, when the site was acquired by the present owners, there was no evidence of the once glorious garden. According to them, bit by bit, original flagstone surfaces were unearthed, stone walls restored, gardens dug and flowers planted, creating once again a sunken garden within the stone walled perimeter. The garden is readily accessible from the street where the public can enter freely. The essence of the garden is the serenity within its stone-walled cruciform shape, surrounded by natural, steeply sloped woodlands.

**GARDEN WITH TIBETAN
PRAYER FLAGS**
Private residence
Bloomingdale

Barry Lobdell ◆ Map #3

"Our sacred space is of a personal nature," says this garden's creator. "Influenced and inspired by world cultures, the resulting space touches people in a harmonious and peaceful way—evoking feelings of comfort and pleasure. One such culture, which has inspired us deeply with its peace, compassion, and strength, is that of the Tibetans. The Tibetan prayer flags, or wind horses as they are also known, are prominently displayed. Waving in the wind, they bless our space with hundreds of mantras and prayers that permeate throughout our community and radiate out into the world."

71

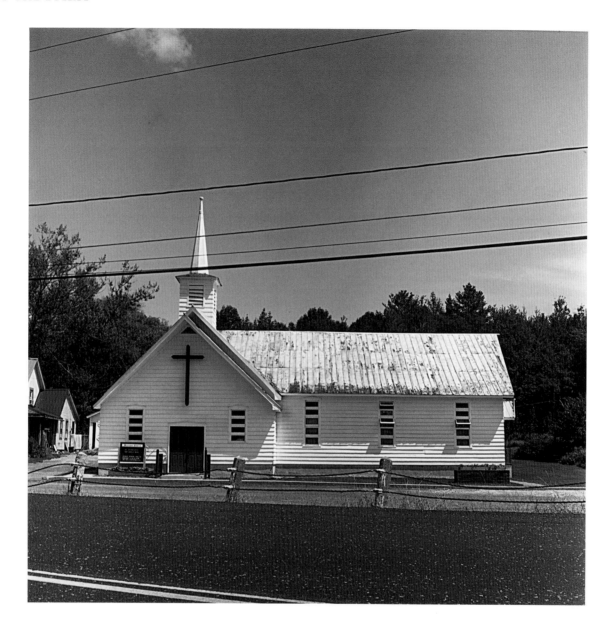

BAKERS MILLS WESLEYAN
CHURCH
Bakers Mills
Built 1891

Heather MacLeod ◆ *Map #2*

This church, the oldest in the hamlet of Bakers Mills, was expanded in 1964 with materials from the recently demolished Johnsburg Wesleyan Methodist. The original portion was built from logs skidded by local men and cut by John P. Baker, for whose sawmill Bakers Mills is named. The pastor at the time, the Reverend J.J. Davison, was a skilled carpenter and led the construction efforts.

WEVERTOWN UNITED
METHODIST CHURCH
Wevertown
Built 1879

Shellburne Thurber ◆ Map #32

Wevertown is one of four hamlets in the Town of Johnsburg to build its own Methodist church in the nineteenth century. Today all four of those historic buildings remain, but they comprise one parish, served by one minister. The tall windows down each side of the church are memorials to past members. The Adirondack Ensemble now makes its home here and uses the sanctuary as a performance space.

FORMER CHURCH OF THE REDEEMER
(Now an antique shop)
Bloomingdale
Built 1882

Barry Lobdell ◆ *Map #3*

Originally a seasonal church funded and primarily used by summer people, the building fell out of use by the 1930s. The original stained glass and fixtures were removed by scavengers and the building was eventually condemned. A local businessman rented and then purchased the building in the mid-1970s, saving it from demolition. Much of the original white oak interior remains. Other notable features include the bell tower at a 45-degree angle to the building, the scissor-truss roof supports, and the cut-out work in the gables.

Church of the Redeemer was built by Ben Muncil, who also worked on White Pine Camp (see page 43).

VAN SANTVOORD ROOM
Keene Valley Community Church
Keene Valley
Built 1878

Shellburne Thurber ◆ Map #16

"Our church enjoys a lively, active congregation and is used not only for regular worship services, weddings, funerals and vigils, but for concerts, recitals, theatrical performances, lectures and readings," says a parishioner. *"It is truly the focal point of the community."* The Van Santvoord Room was built between 1928 and 1931, when the artist Ray Strong initially painted the superb 270 degree mural depicting the mountains surrounding Keene Valley. Strong touched up his work in 1955, and in 2004 a professional restorer will repair damage sustained over the years.

FORMER ST. CHARLES
BORROMEO CHURCH
(Now Orvis Outfitters)
Wevertown
Built 1875, used as a church until 1980

Heather MacLeod • Map #32

Built in 1897 to serve Irish and French immigrants who came to the Adirondacks to work in nearby mills and tanneries, this church has been adapted for other uses. Nonetheless, signs of the sacred remain here. Computers and office equipment fill the former choir loft; snowshoes hang where an altar once stood; and as in many places of worship with high, vaulted ceilings, one's eyes are always drawn skyward.

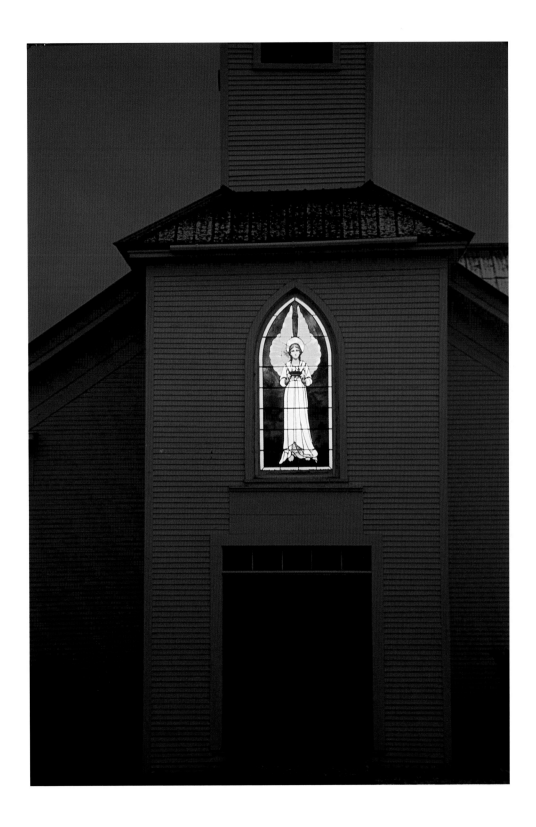

CHURCH OF THE NAZARENE
Vermontville
Built 1856

Barry Lobdell ◆ Map #30

The angel in the stained glass window, made in 1776 in Denmark, was a gift from a demolished church in Deerland, New York. In a history of the window, one worshipper said that this angel "saw couples get married, have their babies baptized, and finally be buried in dignity... It could tell of many scenes of happiness and sorrow... of generous offers to help other... of human beings at their best and worst; of war and peace, of drowsy summer afternoons and winter days of storm and fighting. And the angel looked on in blessing..."

ABOUT THE PHOTOGRAPHERS

Barry Lobdell lives in the village of Saranac Lake, in the heart of the Adirondack Park in northern New York State. His current photographic interests center around the mountain landscape that surrounds him. He works with both standard format and panoramic cameras, utilizing film as a starting point, then scanning images into the digital environment, where they are edited, refined and printed.

His introduction to photography came while he was a university student in the early 1970s, and he has pursued it creatively ever since. He is a member of the Adirondack Artists Guild, which consists of a group of 11 artists living and working in and around Saranac Lake.

His photographs are on continuing display at the Artists Guild gallery in Saranac Lake, and Barry's work is held in many private and public collections. His photographs have been honored in both national and regional competitions and have been published in many forms throughout his career.

Heather MacLeod lives in Halifax, Nova Scotia and says her first notion of 'self' came at four years of age after seeing a portrait photograph of herself taken by a family friend who was a professional photographer. She still can recall the intense heat and blinding brightness of the studio lights and the tension of maintaining a constant smile for the photographer during that shoot. When she saw the resulting image of herself on an eight by ten inch sheet of glossy black and white paper she was surprised by what had been captured. Was that really her?

She continues to be surprised by photography. After buying her first camera, in the late 1970s, she studied photography at the Nova Scotia College of Art and Design—followed by cultural / environmental studies and teaching. Her work has explored nature / culture dynamics relating to landscape perception, sense of place and the identity of belonging. In particular, this documentary photography has focused on symbolic structures, objects and icons that have a strong archetypal resonance in the landscape.

Her recent work has examined the frontier mythology evident in the landscape of the Canadian west, the lighthouse icon in the landscape of the Canadian east as represented by the folk tradition of lawn lighthouses at the end of driveways, and archways in public and private landscapes that function as symbolic passages demarcating memory and place.

Romaine Orthwein is a graduate of New York University and is currently pursuing an MFA at the School of Visual Arts in New York. Her work has appeared in such publications as *Esquire, Think, Glue,* and *Afterimage.* Among her other credits are poster art for feature films *Brown's Requiem* and *Hugo Pool* and publicity photos for *Thick as Thieves.* More than one hundred of Orthwein's photos were featured in the documentary *Dominique Dunne: An American Tragedy.* She has had solo exhibitions at the Miller/Geisler Gallery in New York and the Nicole Dintaman Gallery in Los Angeles and has participated in group exhibitions at Westside Gallery, A.I.R. Gallery, and Exit Art, all in New York, and at the Gallery 510 Arts Guild in Illinois.

Shellburne Thurber is an artist, commercial photographer and adjunct photography instructor. She has exhibited widely both in the United States and abroad, including group shows at the Aldrich Museum in Ridgefield, CT, Real Art Ways in Hartford, CT, the Fogg Art Museum at Harvard University, the Worcester Art Museum in Worcester, MA, Thread Waxing Space in New York City, the McMullen Museum at Boston College, the DeCordova Museum and Sculpture Park in Lincoln, MA, as well as shows in Argentina, Belgium, and France.

In 1996, Thurber was one of the first women to be awarded the Anonymous Was A Woman grant. In 1999, she was awarded a Bunting Fellowship at the Radcliffe Institute for Advanced Study, Harvard University. Her fellowship included a one-person show in March of 2000. She continued at the Bunting as an affiliate fellow for the year 2000/2001. She was artist in residence for three years at the Boston Athenaeum starting in 1999 and ending this past fall with a one-person show in the newly renovated library. This exhibition included a film and a 75-page full-color catalogue.

In the fall of 2000, Thurber was awarded the Maud Morgan prize by the Museum of Fine Arts, Boston. This prize is given yearly to one-woman artist from the Boston area and includes an exhibition of the recipient's work at the Museum. Thurber lectures frequently as a visiting artist in schools throughout the northeast, including the Massachusetts College of Art, the Boston Museum School, Rhode Island School of Design and Tufts University. She has also taught as an adjunct photography instructor at both the Massachusetts College of Art and Tufts University.

EXHIBITION PHOTOGRAPHS

BARRY LOBDELL

Interior, St. Brendan's Catholic Church, Keene, 2001
lightjet print; 30 X 20"

Duane Methodist Church, 2001
lightjet print; 30 X 20"

Soldier's Monument, Wevertown, 2001
lightjet print; 30 X 20"

Teahouse, White Pine Camp, Paul Smiths, 2001
lightjet print; 30 X 20"

Church of the Nazarene, Vermontville, 2001
lightjet print; 30 X 20"

Garden with Tibetan Prayer Flags, Bloomingdale, 2001
lightjet print; 30 X 20"

Interior, Memorial Presbyterian, Childwold, 2001
lightjet print; 30 X 20"

Former Church of the Redeemer, Bloomingdale, 2002
lightjet print; 30 X 20"

HEATHER MACLEOD

North Creek First Baptist Church, 2001
chromogenic print; 30 x 30"

Former St. Charles Borromeo Church, Wevertown,
2001; chromogenic print; 30 x 30"

Former Episcopal Summer Church, Gabriels, 2001
chromogenic print; 30 x 30"

Bakers Mills Wesleyan Church, 2001
chromogenic print; 30 x 30"

Log Cabin Church, Mayfield, 2001
chromogenic print; 30 x 30"

Virgin Mary Shrine, Keene, 2001
chromogenic print; 30 x 30"

St. John's in the Wilderness, Paul Smiths, 2001
(St. John the Baptist Statue)
chromogenic print; 30 x 30"

Pottersville United Methodist Church, 2001
chromogenic print; 30 x 30"

Good Shepherd Episcopal Church, Chestertown, 2001
chromogenic print; 30 x 30"

Church of the White Fathers of Africa, Lake Kushaqua,
2001; chromogenic print; 30 x 30"

ROMAINE ORTHWEIN

Untitled, (Tapawingo Chapel, Lake Placid),
2002; chromogenic print; 20 x 24"

Untitled, (Interior, Beth Joseph Synagogue,
Tupper Lake), 2002; chromogenic print;
20 x 24"

Untitled, (United Church of Christ,
Elizabethtown), 2002
chromogenic print; 20 x 24"

Untitled, (Uihlein Mercy Center, Lake Placid),
2002; chromogenic print; 20 x 24"

Untitled, (Chapel Island, Exterior from Interior,
Upper Saranac Lake), 2002
chromogenic print; 20 x 24"

Untitled, (Chapel Island, Exterior, Upper
Saranac Lake), 2002; chromogenic print;
20 x 24"

Untitled, (Camp Dudley Outdoor Chapel,
Westport), 2002; chromogenic print; 20 x 24"

Untitled, (St. Eustace Episcopal Church, Lake
Placid), 2002; chromogenic print; 20 x 24"

Untitled, (St. James Episcopal Church, Au Sable
Forks), 2002; chromogenic print; 20 x 24"

Untitled, (Interior, St. Brendan's Catholic
Church, Keene), 2002;
chromogenic print; 20 x 24"

Untitled, (St. Brendan's Confession Booth,
Keene), 2002; chromogenic print; 20 x 24"

Untitled, (Private Garden, Original Site of
St. Eustace-by-the-Lakes Episcopal Church)
2002; chromogenic print; 20 x 24"

SHELLBURNE THURBER

Child's Grave, Duane, New York, 2002
chromogenic print; 40 X 40"

Interior, Duane Methodist Church, 2001
chromogenic print; 40 X 40"

Interior, Essex Senior Center, 2001
chromogenic print; 40 X 40"

Van Santvoord Room, Keene Valley Community Church,
2001; chromogenic print; 40 X 40"

Private Chapel, Lower St. Regis Lake, 2001
chromogenic print; 40 X 40"

Interior, St. Michael's Roman Catholic Church, Witherbee,
2001; chromogenic print; 40 X 40"

Interior, Church of All Saints, Mineville, 2001
chromogenic print; 40 X 40"

Interior, Pottersville Christ Episcopal Church, 2001
chromogenic print; 40 X 40"

Interior, Wevertown United Methodist Church, 2001
chromogenic print; 40 X 40"

CHILD'S GRAVE
Duane

Shellburne Thurber ◆ *Map #8*

SITE LOCATIONS

Massena

Malone

Plattsburgh

Potsdam

11

L. Champlain

Keeseville

8

7

17

23

30

29

12

3

11

33

1

34

13

Essex

10

Raquette R.

Upper Saranac L.

28

18

Saranac Lake

Lake Placid

15

16

9

31

6

27

Tupper Lake

87

35

20

Tupper L.

22

Blue Mt. Lake

9

Old Forge

4

Ticonderoga

25

Fulton Chain L.s

Indian L.

21

24

26

5

2

32

L. George

14

Warrensburg

Whitehall

Glens Falls

Hudson Falls

Fort Edward

Great Sacandaga L.

19

Mohawk R.

Saratoga Springs